MW00569661

Love Donuts

Discover deliciously divine
donut recipes

First published in 2013
LOVE FOOD is an imprint of Parragon Books Ltd

Parragon
Chartist House
15-17 Trim Street
Bath, BA1 1HA, UK

www.parragon.com/lovefood

ISBN: 978-1-4723-0206-9

Printed in China

Photography by Mike Cooper
Home economy by Sumi Glass
New recipes and introduction by Angela Drake
Edited by Fiona Biggs

Notes for the Reader
This book uses standard kitchen measuring spoons and cups. All spoon and cup measurements are level unless otherwise indicated. Unless otherwise stated, milk is assumed to be whole, butter is assumed to be salted, eggs are large, individual vegetables are medium, and pepper is freshly ground black pepper. Unless otherwise stated, all root vegetables should be washed and peeled before using.

Garnishes and serving suggestions are all optional and not necessarily included in the recipe ingredients or method. The times given are only an approximate guide. Preparation times differ according to the techniques used by different people, and the cooking times may also vary from those given. Optional ingredients, variations, or serving suggestions have not been included in the calculations.

Recipes using raw or very lightly cooked eggs should be avoided by infants, the elderly, pregnant women, and people with weakened immune systems. Pregnant and breast-feeding women are advised to avoid eating peanuts and peanut products. People with nut allergies should be aware that some of the prepared ingredients used in the recipes in this book may contain nuts. Always check the packaging before use.

Contents

Divine Donuts

Smothered in a delicious, sticky sweet glaze, dipped in chocolate, filled with cream, custard, or jelly, or simply warm and dusted with sugar, freshly made donuts are the ultimate sweet treat—not exactly for every day but certainly for a special occasion. This book is filled with all you need to know about donuts, with 32 recipes from around the world, including all the classics as well as baked donuts, cake donuts, and savory ones!

So why not treat your family and friends by trying one or more of these fabulous donut recipes? You'll be surprised at just how easy they are to make!

TYPES OF DONUTS

YEAST—this is the most popular type of donut. It is made with soft bread dough, usually lightly sweetened with sugar. The dough is kneaded until smooth and left in a warm place to rise before shaping and frying to get that wonderful light and open texture. This type of dough is nearly always fried.

CAKE—a quick and easy cake batter is used to make this type of donut. There's no need to knead the dough or let it rise; simply roll it out, shape it, and fry. This type of batter will result in a donut with a closer texture than a yeasted donut and a crispier crust.

BAKED CAKE—a light cake batter is used for this type of donut. To get the perfect ring donut shape, you will need to invest in a donut pan (see essential equipment). This donut has a much lighter sponge cake texture and is quick to make. It will keep for 2–3 days and is less calorific than a fried donut.

CHURROS—made with choux pastry dough that is usually either piped or dropped into hot oil for frying. This type of donut has a much lighter and more open texture than yeast or cake donuts. It takes just minutes to make and cook—perfect when you want that fried donut fix.

ESSENTIAL EQUIPMENT

DONUT/COOKIE CUTTERS—if you plan to make a lot of ring donuts, consider buying a donut cutter. This handy gadget stamps the donut shape in one swift action. However, it's almost as easy to use two round cookie cutters—one about 3¼ inches in diameter and one measuring about 1 inch—to cut out the holes.

LARGE DEEP PAN OR DEEP-FRYER—a deep-fryer with a built-in temperature gauge makes frying donuts really easy, however, there's no need to rush out and buy one. A medium, deep heavy saucepan that can be filled to a 3¼-inch depth with oil is perfectly suitable and easier to clean.

ELECTRIC MIXER—an electric mixer takes the work out of making donuts. It comes with a paddle attachment for mixing and a dough hook for kneading.

THERMOMETER—a candy thermometer will help make sure that you heat the oil to the correct temperature for frying. It needs to be made of brass or other metal and measure up to a temperature of at least 400°F.

DONUT PANS—for baked cake donuts, you'll need a donut pan that has 6 or 12 molded donut ring-shape cups. The batter is piped or spooned into the cups before baking in the oven. You can also buy miniature donut pans that are ideal for bite-size sweet treats.

PASTRY BAG AND TIPS—for piping churros into hot oil or filling donut pans with batter, a large pastry bag is useful. Buy a reusable plastic bag or a roll of sturdy disposable bags. A few plain and fluted tips in different sizes are handy, too.

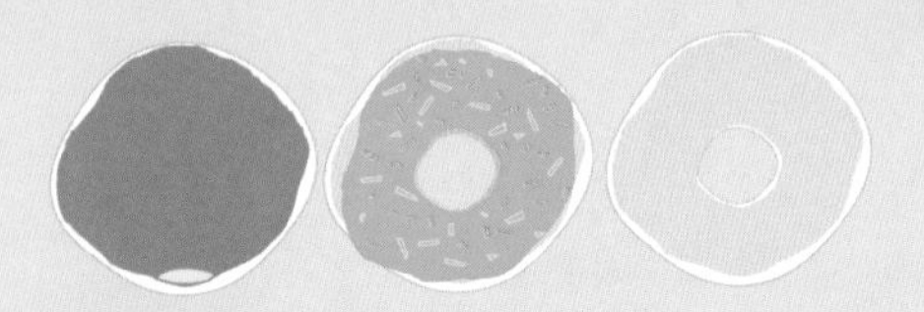

ESSENTIAL INGREDIENTS

You only need a few ingredients for most of the recipes in this book. Here's a guide to some of the basics...

ACTIVE DRY YEAST—unlike fresh or ordinary dry yeast that has to be activated in warm, sweetened liquid before adding to the dry ingredients, active dry yeast is just stirred into the flour. If you use ordinary dried yeast, first mix it with some of the warm liquid and sugar or honey from the recipe and let rest for 15 minutes, until frothy, before adding it to the flour with the rest of the liquid.

FLOUR—for yeast-base donuts, it's vital to use a white bread flour with a high gluten content. This allows for the dough to be kneaded and stretched and will result in a light and airy textured donut. For cake and baked donuts, use all-purpose flour with baking powder or baking soda as the leavening agent.

SUGAR—superfine sugar has a fine texture that dissolves easily and is best for sweetening the donut batter; if you don't have any, process the same amount of granulated sugar in a food processor for 1 minute, or use granulated sugar, although the texture will be slightly different. Use superfine, granulated, or confectioners' sugar to coat the warm, cooked donuts.

OIL—choose a light flavorless oil that can be heated to a high temperature for frying the donuts. Sunflower, peanut, or good-quality vegetable oil are all fine. You can use the same oil for two–three batches of frying, but always strain after each use and discard the oil when it starts to turn a darker color.

EGGS—eggs enrich yeast dough and are essential for a cake or baked dough. Let them reach room temperature before using.

TIPS FOR MAKING YEAST DOUGH

- Don't overheat the liquid—it should be warm but not too hot or it will kill the yeast and the dough won't rise.
- It's better to have a soft, sticky dough and gradually incorporate more flour than a dry and crumbly dough, which will be hard to knead and take longer to rise.
- Once the donuts have been shaped, don't let them sit for too long before frying because they can rise too much and lose their shape.

TIPS FOR FRYING DONUTS

- If you are using a saucepan of oil, don't overfill it—there should be at least 2 inches from the top of the oil to the rim of the pan.
- It's essential to maintain the correct temperature when frying the donuts. If the temperature is too high, they will overbrown but not cook through. If it's too low, the donuts will take longer to cook and absorb more oil, making them soggy and fatty.
- Don't overcrowd the fryer or pan with donuts because this will reduce the temperature of the oil.
- Never leave hot oil unattended because it can be dangerous.

TIPS FOR BAKING DONUTS

- Thoroughly grease the donut pan before use with either softened or melted butter or a cooking spray.
- Don't overfill the cups or you'll lose the donut shape during baking. Piping the batter is the best way to evenly fill the pan, but if the batter has fruit in it, then carefully spoon it in with a teaspoon, wiping away any spills with paper towels.
- Be careful not to overcook baked donuts or they will have a dry texture. The donuts should just spring back when lightly pressed with your fingertips.

Simple Donuts

MAKES 12 · PREP 45 · COOK 25 MINUTES
PLUS RISING & CHILLING

INGREDIENTS

1 cup milk
3 tablespoons active dry yeast
2 cups all-purpose flour, plus extra for dusting
2 tablespoons superfine sugar
½ teaspoon salt
3 egg yolks
1 teaspoon vanilla extract
4 tablespoons butter, softened
oil, for greasing and frying

GLAZE (OPTIONAL)

1½ cups confectioners' sugar
3–4 tablespoons water or milk

1. Heat the milk until lukewarm and dissolve the yeast into the milk. Add 1¾ cups of the flour to the mixture and set aside for 30 minutes.

2. Using an electric mixer fitted with a paddle attachment, add the sugar, salt, egg yolks, and vanilla to the bowl, and mix on low speed until smooth. Add the butter and milk mixture and mix slowly.

3. Change the paddle attachment to a dough hook and add the remaining flour. Mix slowly until the dough is smooth. Refrigerate the dough for 1 hour.

4. Lightly grease a baking sheet. Roll out the dough on a floured surface to about ½ inch thick. Use a donut cutter to cut out the donuts.

5. Place on the greased baking sheet, cover with plastic wrap, and set aside in a warm place. The donuts should rise to nearly double the original size and spring back when touched.

6. Heat enough oil for deep-frying in a large saucepan or deep-fryer to 350–375°F, or until a cube of bread browns in 30 seconds. Carefully place the donuts, one at a time, into the hot oil. Fry for 2 minutes, or until golden brown. Remove with a slotted spoon and drain on paper towels.

7. To make the glaze, place the sugar in a bowl and slowly mix in the water or milk until smooth. Pour over the cooled donuts.

Simple yet delicious, these classic donuts are the perfect treat, with or without the glaze.

Jelly Donuts

MAKES 10 | PREP 25 PLUS RISING | COOK 25 MINUTES

INGREDIENTS

oil, for greasing and frying

3¼ cups white bread flour, plus extra for dusting

4 tablespoons butter, cut into pieces

2 tablespoons superfine sugar

½ teaspoon salt

2¼ teaspoons active dry yeast

1 egg, lightly beaten

¾ cup lukewarm milk

FILLING

½ cup strawberry, grape, or raspberry jelly

1. Lightly grease a large bowl and two baking sheets.

2. Place the flour in a large bowl, add the butter, and rub it in until the mixture resembles bread crumbs. Stir in the sugar, salt, and yeast. Make a well in the center and add the egg and milk, then mix to form a soft, pliable dough. Knead well for 10 minutes.

3. Place in the greased bowl and cover. Set aside in a warm place to rise for about 1 hour, or until doubled in size.

4. Knead the dough on a floured work surface, then divide into ten pieces. Shape each piece into a ball and place on the prepared baking sheets. Cover and set aside in a warm place to double in size for 45 minutes.

5. Heat enough oil for deep-frying in a large saucepan or deep-fryer to 350–375°F, or until a cube of bread browns in 30 seconds. Deep-fry the donuts in batches for 2–3 minutes each side. Remove with a slotted spoon, drain on paper towels, and dust with sugar.

6. To fill the donuts, spoon the jelly into a pastry bag fitted with a plain tip. Insert a sharp knife into each donut and twist to make a hole. Push the point of the tip into the hole and pipe in some jelly.

Why not try blueberry or apricot preserves—or any other type of Jelly, Jam, or preserves you like—for a different taste experience.

Baked Ring Donuts

MAKES 16 PREP 20 COOK 45 MINUTES

INGREDIENTS

1¾ cups all-purpose flour
4 teaspoons baking powder
¾ cup superfine sugar
½ teaspoon salt
⅔ cup milk
2 eggs, beaten
½ teaspoon vanilla extract
3 tablespoons butter, melted, plus extra for greasing

SUGAR COATING

¼ cup superfine sugar
2–3 teaspoons ground cinnamon

1. Preheat the oven to 375°F. Grease a 6-cup donut pan.

2. Sift together the flour and baking powder into a bowl and stir in the sugar and salt. Make a well in the center. Mix together the milk, eggs, vanilla extract, and butter and pour into the well. Mix until smooth.

3. Spoon the batter into a large pastry bag fitted with a plain tip. Pipe some of the batter into the prepared pan, filling each cup about two-thirds full. Bake in the preheated oven for 10–15 minutes, or until risen, golden, and just firm to the touch. Let cool in the pan for 5 minutes, then turn out onto a wire rack. Bake the remaining batter in the same way, rinsing and greasing the pan each time, to make 16 donuts in total.

4. To make the sugar coating, mix together the sugar and cinnamon on a plate. Gently toss each warm donut in the cinnamon sugar to coat completely. Serve warm or cold.

Made with a simple cake batter instead of yeast dough, these baked donuts have a wonderful, light texture and will keep fresh for longer than deep-fried donuts.

Custard Donuts

MAKES **8**
PREP **45** PLUS RISING
COOK **20** MINUTES

INGREDIENTS

¾ cup milk
2 tablespoons butter
2½ cups white bread flour, plus extra for dusting and kneading
½ teaspoon salt
1½ teaspoons active dry yeast
2 tablespoons superfine sugar, plus extra for coating
1 egg, beaten
oil, for deep-frying and greasing
¼ cup raspberry jelly

CUSTARD FILLING

2 eggs
¼ cup superfine sugar
1 teaspoon vanilla extract
3 tablespoons cornstarch
2 cups milk

1. Put the milk and butter into a small saucepan over low heat and heat until the butter has melted. Let cool for 5 minutes.

2. Sift the flour into a large bowl and stir in the salt, yeast, and sugar. Pour in the milk mixture and the egg and mix to a soft dough. Turn out the dough onto a floured surface and knead for 5–6 minutes, until smooth and elastic, adding a little more flour, if needed.

3. Put the dough into a bowl, cover, and set aside in a warm place for 1 hour, or until doubled in size. Line two large baking sheets with parchment paper.

4. Briefly knead the dough and divide into eight pieces. Shape each piece into a 5-inch length. Place on the prepared baking sheets and cover with lightly oiled plastic wrap. Set aside in a warm place for 10–15 minutes, until puffy.

5. Heat enough oil for deep-frying in a large saucepan or deep-fryer to 350–375°F, or until a cube of bread browns in 30 seconds. Add the donuts, two or three at a time, and fry on each side for 1–2 minutes, or until golden. Remove and drain on paper towels, then toss in sugar to coat. Let cool.

6. To make the filling, put the eggs, sugar, vanilla extract, and cornstarch into a bowl and beat together until smooth. Put the milk into a saucepan over medium heat and heat until almost boiling, then beat it into the egg mixture. Return the custard to the pan and cook, beating continuously, for 8–10 minutes, until smooth and thickened. Transfer to a bowl, cover the surface with wax paper, and let cool completely.

7. Split the donuts lengthwise and spread jelly down the center of each one. Spoon the custard into a large pastry bag fitted with a star-shape tip and pipe the custard on top of the jelly.

Split and filled with jelly and custard, these donuts make the perfect coffee break treat. You can use store-bought vanilla pudding or whipped cream instead, if you prefer.

Lemon Crullers

MAKES 16 **PREP** 40 PLUS RISING **COOK** 15 MINUTES

INGREDIENTS

¾ cup milk

2 tablespoons butter

2½ cups white bread flour, plus extra for dusting and kneading

½ teaspoon salt

1½ teaspoons active dry yeast

3 tablespoons superfine sugar

2 teaspoons finely grated lemon rind

1 egg, beaten

oil, for deep-frying and greasing

GLAZE

1⅓ cups confectioners' sugar

¼ cup lemon juice

1. Put the milk and butter into a small saucepan over low heat and heat until the butter has melted. Let cool for 5 minutes.

2. Sift the flour into a large bowl and stir in the salt, yeast, sugar, and lemon rind. Pour in the milk mixture and the egg and mix to a soft dough. Turn out the dough onto a floured surface and knead for 5–6 minutes, until smooth and elastic, adding a little more flour, if needed. Put the dough into a bowl, cover, and set aside in a warm place for 1 hour, or until doubled in size. Line two large baking sheets with parchment paper.

3. Briefly knead the dough and roll out to a 10 x 12½-inch rectangle. Cut the dough into 16 short strips and tightly twist each strip two or three times. Place the donuts on the prepared baking sheets and cover with lightly oiled plastic wrap. Set aside in a warm place for 10 minutes, until puffy.

4. Heat enough oil for deep-frying in a large saucepan or deep-fryer to 350–375°F, or until a cube of bread browns in 30 seconds. Add the donuts, two or three at a time, and fry on each side for 1–2 minutes, or until golden. Remove with a slotted spoon and drain on paper towels.

5. To make the glaze, mix together the confectioners' sugar and lemon juice until smooth. When the donuts are just cool enough to handle, dip each one in the lemon glaze to coat. Let set on a wire rack.

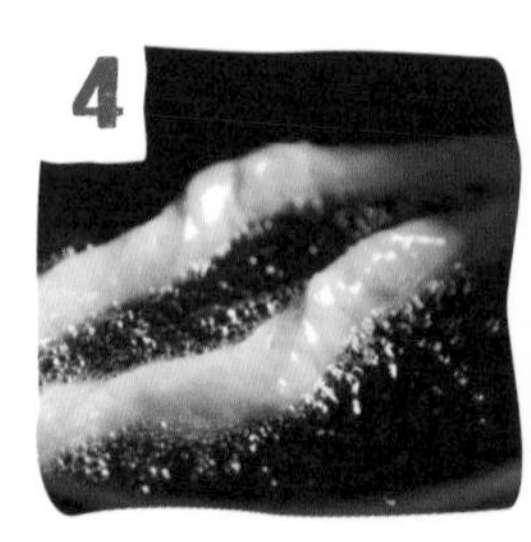

These short twists of dough with a lemon glaze are simple to make. Don't worry if they untwist a little when fried—they will still taste delicious!

Coconut Donuts

MAKES **12** PREP **20** COOK **30** MINUTES

INGREDIENTS

1⅓ cups all-purpose flour
1 tablespoon baking powder
½ cup superfine sugar
¼ teaspoon salt
⅔ cup coconut milk
1 egg, lightly beaten
2 tablespoons butter, melted, plus extra for greasing
1⅓ cups unsweetened flaked dried coconut
⅓ cup raspberry or grape jelly, warmed

1. Preheat the oven to 375°F. Grease a 6-cup donut pan.

2. Sift together the flour and baking powder into a bowl and stir in the sugar and salt. Make a well in the center. Mix together the coconut milk, egg, and butter, pour into the well, and mix until smooth. Stir in ⅓ cup of the coconut.

3. Spoon the batter into a large pastry bag fitted with a plain tip. Pipe half the batter into the donut cups. Bake in the preheated oven for 10–15 minutes, until risen, golden, and just firm to the touch. Let cool in the pan for 5 minutes, then turn out onto a wire rack. Rinse and regrease the donut pan and repeat with the remaining batter to make 12 donuts in total.

4. Sprinkle the remaining coconut over a large, flat plate. Brush the warm donuts all over with the warm jelly and dip in the coconut to coat completely. Serve warm or cold.

These light-as-air baked donuts are brushed with warm jelly, then smothered in dried coconut. To give them a nuttier flavor, first lightly toast the coconut.

Apple Donuts

MAKES 16 | PREP 40 PLUS RISING | COOK 20 MINUTES

INGREDIENTS

1¼ cups milk
3 tablespoons butter
3¾ cups white bread flour, plus extra for dusting and kneading
½ teaspoon salt
2 teaspoons active dry yeast
¼ cup superfine sugar
2 teaspoons ground cinnamon
1 extra-large egg, beaten
1 large Pippin apple, peeled, cored, and diced
oil, for deep-frying and greasing

GLAZE

1 cup confectioners' sugar
1 teaspoon ground cinnamon
2 tablespoons milk

1. Put the milk and butter into a small saucepan over low heat and heat until the butter has melted. Let cool for 5 minutes.

2. Sift the flour into a large bowl and stir in the salt, yeast, sugar, and cinnamon. Pour in the milk mixture and egg and mix to a soft dough. Turn out onto a floured surface and knead for 5–6 minutes, until smooth and elastic, adding a little more flour, if needed. Flatten the dough, spoon the diced apple over it, and knead into the dough for 2 minutes.

3. Place the dough in a bowl, cover, and set aside in a warm place for 1 hour, or until doubled in size. Line two large baking sheets with parchment paper.

4. Briefly knead the dough and roll out on a floured surface to a thickness of ½ inch. Use a 3¼-inch round cutter to stamp out 12 donuts. Lightly reknead the scraps, roll out, and stamp out another 4 donuts. Place the donuts on the prepared baking sheets and cover with lightly oiled plastic wrap. Set aside in a warm place for 10 minutes, until puffy.

5. Heat enough oil for deep-frying in a large saucepan or deep-fryer to 350–375°F, or until a cube of bread browns in 30 seconds. Add the donuts, a few at a time, and fry on each side for 1–2 minutes, or until golden. Remove with a slotted spoon and drain on paper towels.

6. To make the glaze, put the confectioners' sugar, cinnamon, and milk into a bowl and mix together until smooth. When the donuts are just cool enough to handle, dip the top of each in the glaze. Transfer to a wire rack to set.

Chunks of sweet apple and ground cinnamon give these deep-fried donuts a wonderful spiced fruit flavor. They are best eaten warm, Just after the glaze has set.

Beignets

MAKES **30** PREP **35** PLUS RISING COOK **25** MINUTES

INGREDIENTS

½ cup lukewarm water
2 teaspoons active dry yeast
¼ cup superfine sugar
½ teaspoon salt
1 egg, beaten
¾ cup evaporated milk, warmed
3¼ cups white bread flour, plus extra for dusting and kneading
2 tablespoons vegetable shortening, softened
oil, for deep-frying
½ cup confectioners' sugar

1. Put the water into a large bowl and whisk in the yeast. Add the sugar, salt, egg, and evaporated milk and whisk to combine. Stir in half the flour and mix to a smooth batter. Beat in the vegetable shortening. Add the remaining flour and mix to a soft dough.

2. Turn out the dough onto a lightly floured surface and knead for 4–5 minutes, until smooth and elastic, adding a little more flour, if needed. Put the dough into a bowl, cover, and set aside in a warm place for about 2 hours, or until doubled in size.

3. Heat enough oil for deep-frying in a large saucepan or deep-fryer to 350–375°F, or until a cube of bread browns in 30 seconds.

4. Meanwhile, briefly knead the dough and roll out on a lightly floured surface to a thickness of ½ inch. Use a sharp knife to cut the dough into about 30 squares.

5. Add the squares, about four at a time, to the hot oil and fry on each side for 1–2 minutes, or until puffed up and deep golden brown. Baste the top of the beignets during frying by gently spooning hot oil over them—this will help them to puff up. Remove with a slotted spoon and drain on paper towels. Thickly dust with confectioners' sugar and serve immediately.

1

2

4

These puffed up, pillow-shape donuts, generously dusted with confectioners' sugar, are popular in cafes in the French quarter of New Orleans.

Chocolate Cake Donuts

MAKES 14
PREP 25 PLUS RESTING
COOK 55 MINUTES

INGREDIENTS

½ cup milk, warmed
1 egg
1 teaspoon vanilla extract
⅓ cup unsweetened cocoa powder
1¾ cups all-purpose flour
½ teaspoon baking soda
½ teaspoon baking powder
½ teaspoon salt
½ cup superfine sugar
2 tablespoons butter
oil, for frying
fresh raspberries, to garnish

GLAZE

2 ounces semisweet chocolate, broken into pieces
2 ounces white chocolate, broken into pieces

1. Blend together the warmed milk, egg, and vanilla extract in a bowl.

2. Using an electric mixer with a paddle attachment, mix together the cocoa powder, flour, baking soda, baking powder, salt, and sugar. Add the butter and blend. Slowly add the milk, egg, and vanilla. Mix until the dough is smooth and thick and resembles cookie dough.

3. Let the dough rest in the mixer for 20 minutes.

4. Roll out the dough on a floured surface. The dough should be ½ inch thick. Using a donut cutter, stamp out 14 donuts.

5. Heat enough oil for deep-frying in a large saucepan or deep-fryer to 350–375°F, or until a cube of bread browns in 30 seconds. Carefully place the donuts, one at a time, into the oil. Fry for 2 minutes on each side, or until golden brown. Remove with a slotted spoon and drain on paper towels.

6. To make the glaze, melt each of the chocolates separately in heatproof bowls set over saucepans of simmering water. Coat the donuts, drizzling the chocolates in a pattern.

You'll find it hard to stop at just one after trying these absolutely delectable donuts.

S'mores Donuts

MAKES **12** PREP **45** PLUS RISING COOK **16** MINUTES

INGREDIENTS

⅔ cup milk

2 tablespoons vegetable shortening

2¼ cups white bread flour, plus extra for dusting and kneading

¼ teaspoon salt

1½ teaspoons active dry yeast

2 tablespoons superfine sugar, plus extra for coating

1 extra-large egg, beaten

12 small squares semisweet chocolate

48 miniature white marshmallows

oil, for deep frying and greasing

1 small graham cracker, crushed

GLAZE

½ cup confectioners' sugar, sifted

2 tablespoons water

1. Put the milk and vegetable shortening into a small saucepan over low heat and heat until the fat has melted. Let cool for 5 minutes.

2. Sift the flour into a large bowl and stir in the salt, yeast, and sugar. Pour in the milk mixture and the egg and mix to a soft dough. Turn out the dough onto a floured surface and knead for 5–6 minutes, until smooth and elastic, adding a little more flour, if needed.

3. Place the dough in a bowl, cover, and set aside in a warm place for 1 hour, or until doubled in size. Line a large baking sheet with parchment paper.

4. Briefly knead the dough and divide into 12 pieces. Roll out each piece to a 3½-inch circle and place a square of chocolate and four miniature marshmallows in the center. Gather up the dough to enclose the filling, tightly pinching the edges together to seal. Place on the prepared baking sheet, seam side down, and flatten each donut slightly with the palm of your hand. Cover with lightly oiled plastic wrap and set aside in a warm place for 8–10 minutes, until puffy.

5. Heat enough oil for deep-frying in a large saucepan or deep-fryer to 350–375°F, or until a cube of bread browns in 30 seconds. Fry the donuts, three at a time, for 1–2 minutes on each side or until golden. Remove and drain on paper towels.

6. To make the glaze, put the confectioners' sugar and water into a bowl and beat together until smooth. Dip the top of each warm donut in the glaze and sprinkle with the graham cracker crumbs. Serve warm.

The only way to eat these delicious donuts is while they are warm, with the chocolate and marshmallow in in the middle still molten.

Honey & Pistachio Mini Donuts

MAKES 24 | PREP 20 | COOK 20 MINUTES

INGREDIENTS

1 cup all-purpose flour
2 teaspoons baking powder
pinch of salt
4 tablespoons butter, softened, plus extra for greasing
¼ cup superfine sugar
1 egg, beaten
⅓ cup milk
⅓ cup finely chopped pistachio nuts

GLAZE

¾ cup confectioners' sugar
1 tablespoon honey, warmed
2 teaspoons milk

1. Preheat the oven to 375°F. Grease a 12-cup miniature donut pan. Sift together the flour, baking powder, and salt into a bowl.

2. Put the butter and sugar into a bowl and beat together until pale and fluffy. Gradually beat in the egg, then stir in half the flour mixture. Beat in the milk, then fold in the remaining flour mixture and three-quarters of the chopped nuts.

3. Spoon the batter into a large, disposable pastry bag. Snip off the end and pipe half the filling into the donut cups, filling each one about two-thirds full.

4. Bake in the preheated oven for 8–10 minutes, until risen, pale golden, and just firm to the touch. Let cool in the pan for 2–3 minutes, then transfer to a wire rack. Bake the remaining batter in the same way, rinsing and greasing the pan before filling.

5. To make the glaze, sift the confectioners' sugar into a bowl and stir in the warm honey and milk to make a smooth glaze. Dip the top of each donut into the glaze, then sprinkle with the remaining chopped nuts.

These dainty little baked cake donuts are just perfect for serving as an afternoon snack. You can replace the pistachios with walnuts or hazelnuts, if you prefer.

Lemon Churros with Orange Dipping Sauce

MAKES 20 PREP 20 COOK 25 MINUTES

INGREDIENTS

1 stick unsalted butter, diced
1¼ cups water
1 cup all-purpose flour, sifted
large pinch of salt
2 extra-large eggs, beaten
finely grated rind of 1 large lemon
oil, for deep-frying
confectioners' sugar, for dusting

ORANGE SAUCE

1 tablespoon arrowroot
1¼ cups fresh orange juice
3 tablespoons superfine sugar

1. To make the orange sauce, blend the arrowroot to a smooth paste with 2 tablespoons of the orange juice and set aside. Put the remaining juice and the sugar into a small saucepan over low heat and heat until the sugar has dissolved. Add the blended arrowroot and simmer gently, stirring continously, for 4–5 minutes, until just thickened. Remove from the heat, cover, and keep warm.

2. Put the butter and water into a large saucepan over medium heat and heat until the butter has melted. Bring to a boil, remove from the heat, and add the flour and salt. Beat thoroughly until the mixture is smooth and comes away from the side of the pan. Let cool for 5 minutes, then gradually beat in the eggs to make a thick and glossy paste. Beat in the lemon rind.

3. Heat enough oil for deep-frying in a large saucepan or deep-fryer to 350–375°F, or until a cube of bread browns in 30 seconds. Spoon the paste into a large pastry bag fitted with a large star tip and pipe four or five short loops of the paste into the hot oil. Fry, turning frequently, for 2–3 minutes, until crisp and golden. Remove with a slotted spoon and drain on paper towels. Keep warm while frying the remaining mixture.

4. Thickly dust the hot churros with confectioners' sugar and serve immediately with the orange sauce for dipping.

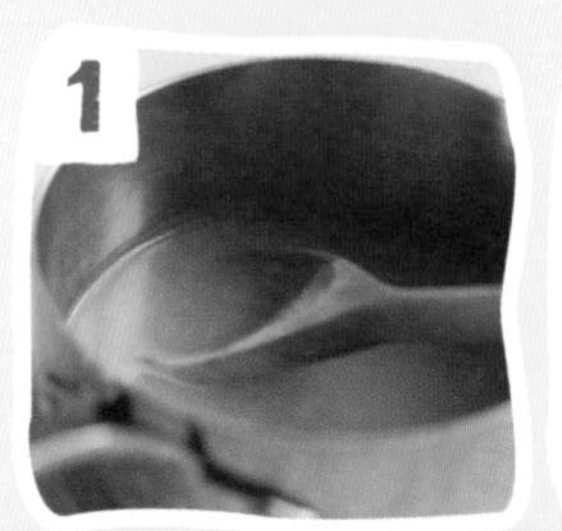

The tangy lemon flavoring means these warm Mexican-style donuts aren't too sweet, even with a generous dusting of confectioners' sugar.

Chocolate-Coated Donut Holes

MAKES 45 PREP 40 COOK 20 MINUTES

PLUS RISING

INGREDIENTS

- ¾ cup milk
- 3 tablespoons butter
- 2¼ cups white bread flour, plus extra for dusting and kneading
- 1 tablespoon unsweetened cocoa powder
- 2 teaspoons ground cinnamon
- ¼ teaspoon salt
- 1½ teaspoons active dry yeast
- 2 tablespoons superfine sugar
- 1 extra-large egg, beaten
- oil, for deep-frying and greasing
- 5 ounces semisweet chocolate, broken into pieces
- 5 ounces white chocolate, broken into pieces
- chocolate or colored sprinkles, to decorate (optional)

1. Put the milk and butter into a small saucepan over low heat and heat until the butter has melted. Leat cool for 5 minutes.

2. Sift together the flour and cocoa powder into a large bowl and stir in the cinnamon, salt, yeast, and sugar. Pour in the milk mixture and the egg and mix to a soft dough. Turn out the dough onto a floured surface and knead for 5–6 minutes, until smooth and elastic, adding a little more flour, if needed.

3. Put the dough into a bowl, cover, and set aside in a warm place for 1 hour, or until doubled in size. Line three baking sheets with parchment paper.

4. Briefly knead the dough and roll out on a lightly floured surface to a thickness of ½ inch. Using a 1-inch cookie cutter, stamp out about 45 disks, rerolling the dough as necessary. Place the disks on two of the prepared baking sheets and cover with lightly oiled plastic wrap. Set aside in a warm place for 5–10 minutes, until puffy.

5. Heat enough oil for deep-frying in a large saucepan or deep-fryer to 350–375°F, or until a cube of bread browns in 30 seconds. Add the disks, six to eight at a time, and fry for 2–3 minutes, until golden, gently turning them in the hot oil all the time. Remove with a slotted spoon and drain on paper towels. Let cool.

6. Put the semisweet chocolate and white chocolate into two separate heatproof bowls set over saucepans of simmering water and heat until melted. Let cool for 5 minutes, then dip half the donut holes in semisweet chocolate to completely coat and dip the remaining holes in white chocolate. Top with chocolate or colored sprinkles, if using. Transfer to the remaining prepared baking sheet and let set.

For some, the best part of the donut is the hole—so why not Just make a whole batch of them? These chocolate-coated ones are perfect for a children's party.

Baked Blueberry Donuts

MAKES 12 PREP 20 COOK 30 MINUTES

INGREDIENTS

1⅔ cups all-purose flour
1 tablespoon baking powder
½ cup superfine sugar
¼ teaspoon salt
½ cup buttermilk
2 extra-large eggs, beaten
½ teaspoon vanilla extract
2 tablespoons butter, melted, plus extra for greasing
1 cup small fresh blueberries

GLAZE

1 cup confectioners' sugar
2 tablespoons milk
1 teaspoon vanilla extract

1. Preheat the oven to 375°F. Grease a 6-cup donut pan.

2. Sift together the flour and baking powder into a bowl and stir in the sugar and salt. Make a well in the center. Put the buttermilk, eggs, vanilla extract, and melted butter into a small bowl, mix together, and pour into the well. Mix until smooth, then gently fold in the blueberries.

3. Using a teaspoon, carefully spoon half the batter into the prepared pan, being careful not to overfill the holes—they should be about two-thirds full. Bake in the preheated oven for 12–15 minutes, or until risen, golden, and just firm to the touch. Let cool in the pan for 5 minutes, then turn out onto a wire rack. Rinse and regrease the pan and repeat with the remaining mixture.

4. To make the glaze, sift the confectioners' sugar into a bowl and beat in the milk and vanilla extract until smooth. Spoon the glaze over the donuts, letting it run down the sides. Let set.

Full of plump, fresh blueberries, these donuts have a wonderful fruity flavor, perfectly complemented by the sweet vanilla glaze.

Cookies & Cream Donuts

MAKES **12** PREP **45** PLUS RISING COOK **20** MINUTES

INGREDIENTS

¾ cup milk
2 tablespoons butter
2½ cups white bread flour, plus extra for dusting and kneading
¼ teaspoon salt
1½ teaspoons active dry yeast
2 tablespoons superfine sugar, plus extra for coating
1 egg, beaten
oil, for deep-frying and greasing
¼ cup raspberry jelly

FILLING

2 cups heavy cream
6 chocolate sandwich cookies, coarsely crushed

GLAZE

1 cup confectioners' sugar
2 tablespoons water

1. Put the milk and butter into a small saucepan over low heat and heat until the butter has melted. Let cool for 5 minutes.

2. Sift the flour into a large bowl and stir in the salt, yeast, and sugar. Pour in the milk mixture and the egg and mix to a soft dough. Turn out the dough onto a floured surface and knead for 5–6 minutes, until smooth and elastic, adding a little more flour, if needed.

3. Put the dough into a bowl, cover, and set aside in a warm place for 1 hour, or until doubled in size. Line two large baking sheets with parchment paper.

4. Briefly knead the dough and roll out on a lightly floured surface to a thickness of ½ inch. Using a 3½-inch donut cutter, stamp out eight donuts. Lightly reknead the scraps, roll out, and stamp out another four donuts. Place on the prepared baking sheets. Cover with lightly oiled plastic wrap and set aside in a warm place for 10 minutes, until puffy.

5. Heat enough oil for deep-frying in a large saucepan or deep-fryer to 350–375°F, or until a cube of bread browns in 30 seconds. Add the donuts, two or three at a time, and fry on each side for 1–2 minutes, or until golden. Remove and drain on paper towels. Let cool.

6. To make the filling, whip the cream until it holds soft peaks. Set aside 2 tablespoons of the crushed cookies and fold the remainder into the cream.

7. To make the glaze, sift the confectioners' sugar into a bowl and beat in the water until smooth.

8. Halve each donut horizontally and spread the jelly on the bottom halves. Spoon the filling on top of the jelly. Dip each top half in the glaze and place on top of the cream filling. Sprinkle with the reserved crushed cookies and let set.

With a wonderful, sweet cream filling, these donuts are perfect for a special occasion. They can be made the day before and kept in the refrigerator overnight.

Rocky Road Donuts

MAKES 8
PREP 40 PLUS RISING
COOK 20 MINUTES

INGREDIENTS

¾ cup milk

3 tablespoons butter

2 cups white bread flour, plus extra for dusting and kneading

2 tablespoons unsweetened cocoa powder

¼ teaspoon salt

1½ teaspoons active dry yeast

2 tablespoons superfine sugar

1 extra-large egg, beaten

oil, for deep-frying and greasing

TOPPING

4 ounces milk chocolate, broken into pieces

3 tablespoons unsalted butter

3 tablespoons chopped mixed nuts

¾ cup miniature pink and white marshmallows

2 tablespoons chopped candied cherries

1. Put the milk and butter into a small saucepan over low heat and heat until the butter has melted. Let cool for 5 minutes.

2. Sift together the flour and cocoa powder into a large bowl and stir in the salt, yeast, and sugar. Pour in the milk mixture and the egg and mix to a soft dough. Turn out the dough onto a floured surface and knead for 5–6 minutes, until smooth and elastic, adding a little more flour, if needed.

3. Put the dough into a bowl, cover, and set aside in a warm place for 1–1½ hours, or until doubled in size. Line a large baking sheet with parchment paper.

4. Briefly knead the dough and roll out on a lightly floured surface to a thickness of ½ inch. Using a 3½-inch donut cutter, stamp out six donuts. Lightly reknead the scraps, roll out, and stamp out another two donuts. Place on the prepared baking sheet. Cover with lightly oiled plastic wrap and set aside in a warm place for 10 minutes, until puffy.

5. Heat enough oil for deep-frying in a large saucepan or deep-fryer to 350–375°F, or until a cube of bread browns in 30 seconds. Add the donuts, a few at a time, and fry on each side for 1–2 minutes, or until golden. Remove with a slotted spoon and drain on paper towels. Let cool.

6. To make the topping, put the chocolate and butter into a heatproof bowl set over a saucepan of gently simmering water and heat until melted. Stir until smooth, then let cool for 5 minutes. Dip each donut in the chocolate glaze and place on a wire rack. Top with the nuts, marshmallows, and cherries and drizzle any remaining chocolate sauce over the top. Let set.

These indulgent chocolate donuts have a smooth milk chocolate glaze and are loaded with nuts, marshmallows, and cherries.

Churros

MAKES **16** PREP **25** COOK **20** MINUTES

INGREDIENTS

1 cup water
6 tablespoons butter or lard, diced
2 tablespoons packed dark brown sugar
finely grated rind of 1 small orange (optional)
pinch of salt
1⅓ cups all-purpose flour, well sifted
1 teaspoon ground cinnamon, plus extra for dusting
1 teaspoon vanilla extract
2 eggs
oil, for deep-frying
superfine sugar, for dusting

1. Heat the water, butter, brown sugar, orange rind, if using, and salt in a heavy saucepan over medium heat until the butter has melted.

2. Add the flour, all at once, the cinnamon, and vanilla extract, then remove the saucepan from the heat and beat rapidly until the mixture pulls away from the side of the saucepan.

3. Let cool slightly, then beat in the eggs, one at a time, beating well after each addition, until the batter is thick and smooth. Spoon into a pastry bag fitted with a wide star tip.

4. Heat enough oil for deep-frying in a deep-fryer or deep saucepan to 350–375°F, or until a cube of bread browns in 30 seconds. Pipe 5-inch lengths about 3 inches apart into the hot oil. Fry for 2–3 minutes, turning frequently until crisp and golden. Remove with a slotted spoon and drain on paper towels. Keep warm while frying the remaining batter.

5. Dust the churros with superfine sugar and cinnamon and serve.

1
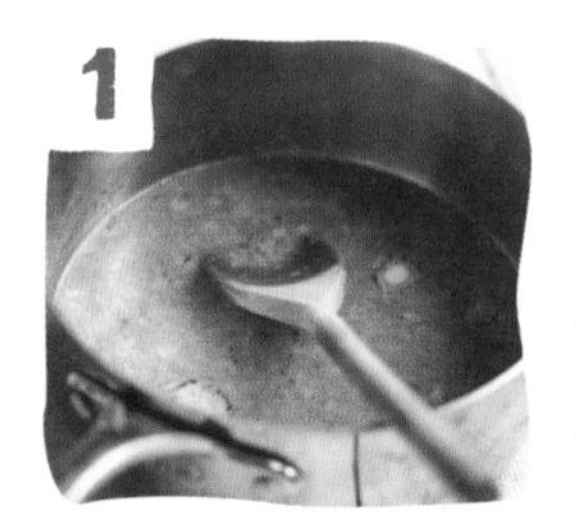

2

4

Served either hot from the saucepan or cooled to room temperature, churros make a delicious treat.

Powdered Donuts

MAKES 8 | PREP 35 PLUS CHILLING | COOK 15 MINUTES

INGREDIENTS

2 cups all-purpose flour, plus extra for dusting
1 tablespoon baking powder
½ teaspoon allspice
¼ teaspoon salt
¼ cup superfine sugar
1 extra-large egg, beaten
½ cup milk
2 tablespoons butter, melted and slightly cooled
½ teaspoon vanilla extract
oil, for deep-frying
1 cup confectioners' sugar, plus extra if needed, for dusting

1. Sift together the flour, baking powder, and allspice into a large bowl. Stir in the salt and sugar. Make a well in the center.

2. Put the egg, milk, butter, and vanilla extract into a bowl, mix together, and pour into the well. Mix to a medium–soft dough, adding a little extra flour if the dough is too sticky to handle. Cover and chill in the refrigerator for 30 minutes.

3. Roll out the dough on a lightly floured surface to a thickness of ½ inch. Use a 3-inch donut cutter to stamp out eight donuts

4. Heat enough oil for deep-frying in a large saucepan or deep-fryer to 350–375°F, or until a cube of bread browns in 30 seconds. Add the donuts, three or four at a time, and fry, turning frequently, for 3–4 minutes, or until crisp and deep golden. Remove and drain on paper towels. Let cool for 10 minutes.

5. Sift the confectioners' sugar into a shallow bowl and toss the donuts in it to coat thoroughly. Serve immediately, before the confectioners' sugar dissolves into the warm donuts—if this does happen, just dust liberally with more confectioners' sugar.

2

3

4

Delicious warm, crisp, and golden fried donuts without having to wait for dough to rise—that's the beauty of these yeast-free donuts.

French Crullers

MAKES **8** PREP **25** PLUS FREEZING COOK **20** MINUTES

INGREDIENTS

4 tablespoons butter
½ cup water
2 teaspoon superfine sugar
1 cup all-purpose flour
1½ teaspoons baking powder
large pinch of salt
2 eggs
1 egg white
oil, for deep-frying

GLAZE

1¾ cups confectioners' sugar
½ cup milk

1. Put the butter, water, and sugar into a large saucepan over medium heat and heat until the butter has melted. Bring to a boil, remove from the heat, and add the flour, baking powder, and salt. Beat thoroughly until the mixture is smooth and comes away from the side of the pan. Return to the heat and cook, stirring continuously, for an additional 1 minute.

2. Let cool for 5 minutes, then gradually beat in the eggs and egg white to make a thick and glossy paste.

3. Line a baking sheet with parchment paper. Spoon the paste into a large pastry bag fitted with a large star tip and pipe eight 3¼-inch rings of the paste onto the prepared baking sheet. Place in the freezer for 1 hour.

4. Heat enough oil for deep-frying in a large saucepan or deep-fryer to 350–375°F, or until a cube of bread browns in 30 seconds. Carefully remove the semifrozen rings from the baking sheet, add to the hot oil in batches of two or three, and fry on each side for 2–3 minutes, until crisp and deep golden brown. Remove with a slotted spoon and drain on paper towels.

5. To make the glaze, sift the confectioners' sugar into a large bowl and beat in the milk until smooth. Dip the warm crullers in the glaze to coat completely and transfer to a wire rack to set.

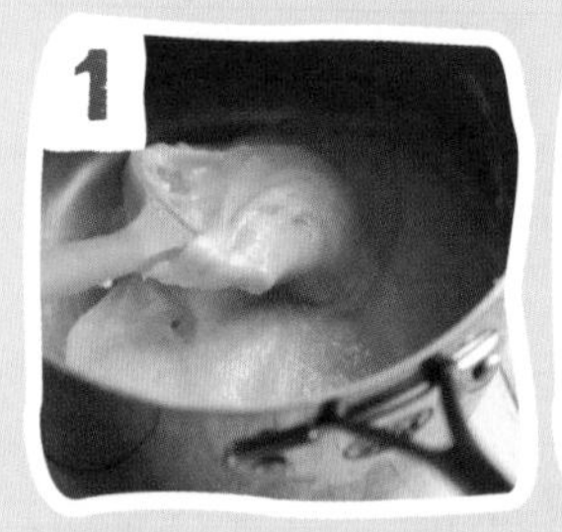

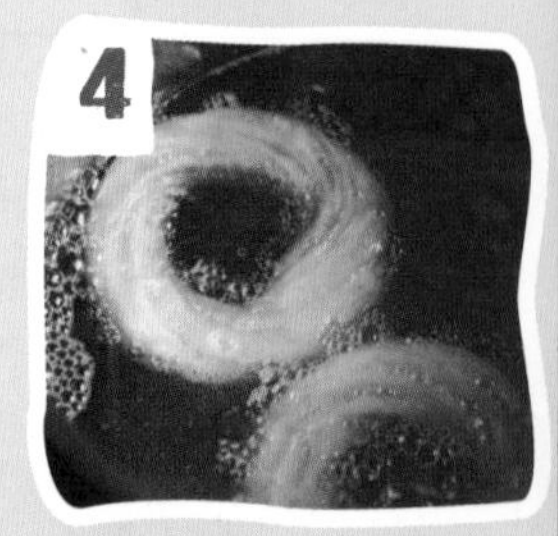

Crisp and golden with a sweet, sticky glaze, these yeast-free donuts are very simple to make. They are best eaten within a few hours of making.

Baked Pumpkin Donuts

MAKES 6 | PREP 25 | COOK 15 MINUTES

INGREDIENTS

1 cup all-purose flour
2 teaspoons baking powder
½ teaspoon salt
1 teaspoon ground cinnamon
½ teaspoon grated nutmeg
3 tablespoons butter, softened, plus extra for greasing
¼ cup packed light brown sugar
1 extra-large egg, beaten
1 teaspoon vanilla extract
1 tablespoon milk
½ cup canned pumpkin puree

GLAZE

1 cup confectioners' sugar
½ teaspoon ground cinnamon
2 tablespoons milk
1–2 teaspoons maple syrup

1. Preheat the oven to 375°F. Grease a 6-cup donut pan.

2. Sift together the flour and baking powder into a bowl and stir in the salt, cinnamon, and nutmeg. Put the butter and brown sugar into a separate bowl and beat together until pale and creamy. Gradually beat in the egg, vanilla extract, and milk. Fold in the flour mixture and pumpkin puree.

3. Spoon the batter into a large pastry bag fitted with a plain tip and pipe into the prepared pan. Bake in the preheated oven for 15 minutes, until risen, golden, and just firm to the touch. Let cool for 5 minutes, then turn out onto a wire rack to cool completely.

4. To make the glaze, sift together the confectioners' sugar and cinnamon into a bowl, add the milk and maple syrup, and stir until smooth. Dip the top of each donut in the glaze and Let set.

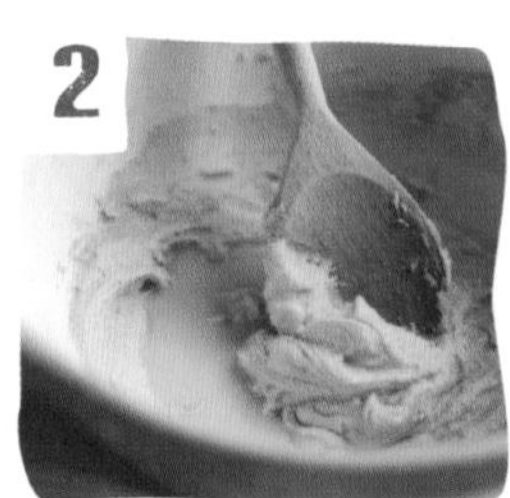

Smooth pumpkin puree gives these light baked donuts a delightful color and delicious moist texture. For a spicier flavor, use ground ginger instead of nutmeg.

Mocha Beignets

MAKES 24 | PREP 40 PLUS RISING | COOK 20 MINUTES

INGREDIENTS

⅓ cup hot strong black coffee
3 tablespoons packed light brown sugar
1½ teaspoons active dry yeast
¼ teaspoon salt
1 egg, beaten
½ cup evaporated milk, warmed
2½ cups white bread flour, plus extra for dusting and kneading
2 tablespoons vegetable shortening, softened
oil, for deep-frying
2 tablespoons finely chopped semisweet chocolate

GLAZE

1 cup confectioners' sugar
1 tablespoon unsweetened cocoa powder
1 tablespoon cold strong black coffee
1–2 tablespoons milk

1. Place the coffee in a large bowl and whisk in the sugar until dissolved. Let cool for 5 minutes, then whisk in the yeast, salt, egg, and evaporated milk. Stir in half the flour and mix to a smooth batter. Beat in the vegetable fat. Add the remaining flour and mix to a soft dough.

2. Turn out the dough onto a lightly floured surface and knead for 4–5 minutes, until smooth and elastic, adding a little more flour, if needed. Place the dough in a bowl, cover, and set aside in a warm place for about 2 hours, or until doubled in size.

3. Heat enough oil for deep-frying in a large saucepan or deep-fryer to 350–375°F, or until a cube of bread browns in 30 seconds.

4. Meanwhile, briefly knead the dough and roll out on a lightly floured surface to a thickness of ½ inch. Use a 2-inch round cookie cutter to stamp out 24 circles, rekneading and rolling the scraps once.

5. Add the circles, about four at a time, to the hot oil and fry on each side for 1–2 minutes, or until puffed up and deep golden brown. Baste the top of the beignets by gently spooning hot oil over them—this will help them to puff up. Remove with a slotted spoon and drain on paper towels.

6. To make the glaze, sift together the confectioners' sugar and cocoa powder into a bowl and stir in the coffee and enough milk to make a smooth glaze. Dip each warm beignet in the glaze and sprinkle with chopped chocolate. Serve immediately.

You can make the dough for these donuts the night before and let it rise slowly in the refrigerator overnight, ready to fry in the morning.

Boston Cream Donuts

MAKES 12
PREP 45 PLUS RISING
COOK 20 MINUTES

INGREDIENTS

¾ cup milk
2 tablespoons butter
2½ cups white bread flour, plus extra for dusting and kneading
½ teaspoon salt
2 tablespoons superfine sugar
1½ teaspoons active dry yeast
1 egg, beaten
oil, for deep-frying and greasing
¼ cup vanilla pudding
½ cup heavy cream, lightly whipped

GLAZE

4 ounce semisweet chocolate, finely chopped
½ cup heavy cream

1. Put the milk and butter into a small saucepan over low heat and heat until the butter has melted. Let cool for 5 minutes.

2. Sift the flour into a large bowl and stir in the salt, sugar, and yeast. Pour in the milk mixture and the egg and mix to a soft dough. Turn out the dough onto a floured surface and knead for 5–6 minutes, until smooth and elastic, adding a little more flour, if needed.

3. Place the dough in a bowl, cover, and set aside in a warm place for 1 hour, or until doubled in size. Line a baking sheet with parchment paper.

4. Briefly knead the dough, divide into 12 pieces, and roll each piece into a ball. Flatten slightly, place on the prepared baking sheet, and cover with lightly oiled plastic wrap. Set aside in a warm place for 10–15 minutes, until puffy.

5. Heat enough oil for deep-frying in a large saucepan or deep-fryer to 350–375°F, or until a cube of bread browns in 30 seconds. Add the donuts to the hot oil, three or four at a time, and fry on each side for 1–2 minutes, or until golden. Remove with a slotted spoon and drain on paper towels. Let cool.

6. Use the tip of a small knife to make a hole in the side of each donut. Push the blade a little way in and move from side to side to create a space. Fold the vanilla pudding into the whipped cream, spoon into a pastry bag with a plain tip, and pipe into the center of the donuts.

7. To make the glaze, put the chocolate into a heatproof bowl set over a saucepan of gently simmering water and heat until melted. Put the cream into a small saucepan over medium heat and heat until almost boiling. Pour it over the chocolate and stir until smooth. Let stand for 5 minutes, then dip the top of each donut in the glaze. Let set.

Based on one of America's favorite cakes, these rich donuts are filled with sweet vanilla cream and have a rich semisweet chocolate glaze.

Maple & Pecan Donuts

MAKES **6**

PREP **45** PLUS RISING

COOK **15** MINUTES

INGREDIENTS

½ cup milk
1 tablespoon butter
3 tablespoons maple syrup
2 cups white bread flour, plus extra for dusting and kneading
¼ teaspoon salt
1½ teaspoons active dry yeast
1 egg, beaten
oil, for deep-frying and greasing
¼ cup finely chopped pecans

FROSTING

¼ cup cream cheese
⅓ cup confectioners' sugar
1 tablespoon maple syrup

1. Put the milk, butter, and maple syrup into a small saucepan over low heat and heat until the butter has melted. Let cool for 5 minutes.

2. Sift the flour into a large bowl and stir in the salt and yeast. Pour in the milk mixture and the egg and mix to a soft dough. Turn out the dough onto a floured surface and knead for 5–6 minutes, until smooth and elastic, adding a little more flour, if needed. Place the dough in a bowl, cover, and set aside in a warm place for 1 hour, or until doubled in size. Line a large baking sheet with parchment paper.

3. Briefly knead the dough and roll out on a lightly floured surface to a 6-x 12-inch rectangle. Use a sharp knife to trim the edges, then cut into six strips. Place on the prepared baking sheet and cover with lightly oiled plastic wrap. Set aside in a warm place for 10–15 minutes, until puffy.

4. Heat enough oil for deep-frying in a large saucepan or deep-fryer to 350–375°F, or until a cube of bread browns in 30 seconds. Add the donuts, two or three at a time, and fry on each side for 1–2 minutes, or until golden. Remove and drain on paper towels. Let cool.

5. For the frosting, beat the cream cheese in a bowl with a wooden spoon until soft, then beat in the confectioners' sugar and maple syrup until smooth. Spread the frosting over the donuts and sprinkle with the chopped pecans.

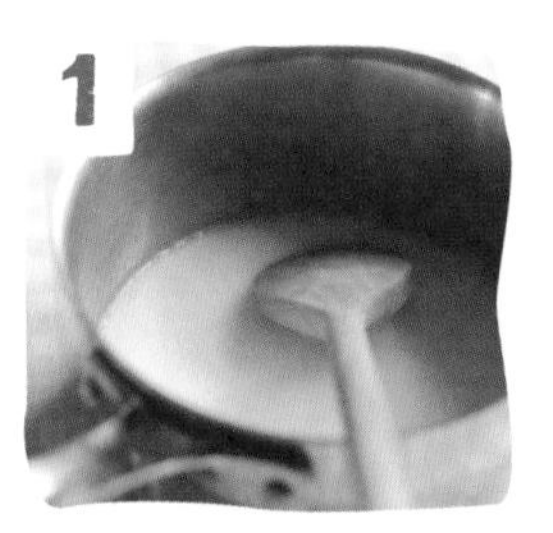
1

3

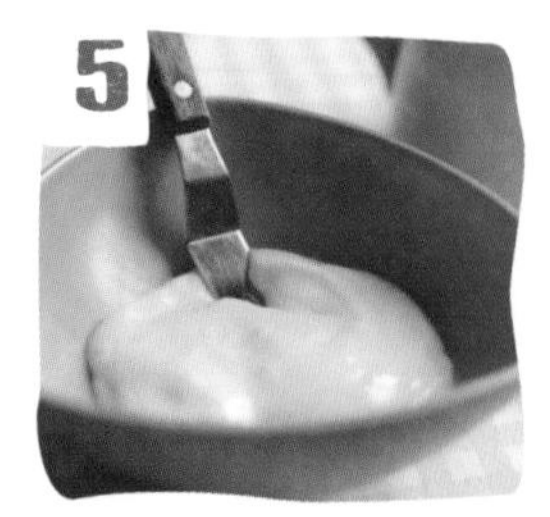
5

These jumbo long donuts are perfect for sharing. For a quirky variation on the topping, sprinkle with chopped crispy bacon instead of the pecans.

Fudge Donuts

MAKES **8** PREP **45** PLUS RISING COOK **25** MINUTES

INGREDIENTS

¾ cup milk
2 tablespoons butter
2½ cups white bread flour, plus extra for dusting and kneading
½ teaspoon salt
1½ teaspoons active yeast
2 tablespoons superfine sugar
1 egg, beaten
oil, for deep-frying and greasing
⅔ cup heavy cream, whipped

FROSTING

4 tablespoons butter
½ cup packed light brown sugar
3 tablespoons milk
1 teaspoon vanilla extract
½ cup confectioners' sugar, sifted

1. Put the milk and butter into a small saucepan over low heat and heat until the butter has melted. Let cool for 5 minutes.

2. Sift the flour into a large bowl and stir in the salt, yeast, and sugar. Pour in the milk mixture and the egg and mix to a soft dough. Turn out the dough onto a floured surface and knead for 5–6 minutes, until smooth and elastic, adding a little more flour, if needed.

3. Put the dough into a bowl, cover, and set aside in a warm place for 1 hour, or until doubled in size. Line a baking sheet with parchment paper.

4. Briefly knead the dough, divide into two pieces and roll out each piece on a lightly floured surface to a 6-inch square. Use a sharp knife to trim the edges, then cut each square into four smaller squares. Place on the prepared baking sheet and cover with lightly oiled plastic wrap. Set aside in a warm place for 10–15 minutes, until puffy.

5. Heat enough oil for deep-frying in a large saucepan or deep-fryer to 350–375°F, or until a cube of bread browns in 30 seconds. Add the donuts, two or three at a time, and fry on each side for 1–2 minutes, or until golden. Remove and drain on paper towels. Let cool.

6. Use the tip of a small knife to make a hole in the side of each donut. Push the blade a little way in and move from side to side to create a space. Spoon the whipped cream into a pastry bag with a plain tip and pipe it into the center of the donuts.

7. To make the frosting, put the butter and brown sugar into a saucepan over medium heat and heat, stirring continuously, until the sugar has dissolved. Bring to a boil and boil for 1 minute, then stir in the milk and vanilla extract. Simmer for an additional 1 minute, then stir in the confectioners' sugar. Let cool for 10–20 minutes, until thickened. Dip each donut in the frosting and let set.

Popular as a sweet treat in Scotland, these square donuts have a whipped cream filling and a delicious, sticky, vanilla-flavored fudge frosting.

Sour Cream Donuts

MAKES	PREP	COOK
24	20	40 MINUTES

INGREDIENTS

1 cup superfine sugar
3 eggs
1 cup sour cream
1 teaspoon vanilla extract
3⅔ cups all-purpose flour, plus extra for dusting and kneading
1 teaspoon baking soda
1 teaspoon baking powder
½ teaspoon salt
¼ teaspoon nutmeg
oil, for frying

GLAZE

1⅔ cups confectioners' sugar
3-4 tablespoons water or milk

1. Beat the sugar and eggs together in a large bowl. Add the sour cream and vanilla extract. Mix well.

2. Add the flour, baking soda, baking powder, salt, and nutmeg and mix well again. Turn out onto a floured board and knead for 5 minutes. The dough should be fairly soft.

3. Roll out the dough to a ¼-inch thickness. Use a floured donut cutter to stamp out 24 donuts.

4. Heat enough oil for deep-frying in a large saucepan or deep-fryer to 350–375°F, or until a cube of bread browns in 30 seconds. Cook the donuts, in batches, by dropping into the hot oil. Fry for 2 minutes, or until golden brown. Remove with a slotted spoon and drain on paper towels.

5. To make the glaze, place the confectioners' sugar in a bowl and slowly mix in the water or milk until smooth.

6. Pour the glaze over the cooled donuts.

This delightful recipe uses sour cream instead of milk,
making them wonderfully light and moist.

Cream Cheese & Herb Donuts

MAKES **16**
PREP **45** PLUS RISING
COOK **20** MINUTES

INGREDIENTS

¾ cup milk

2 tablespoons olive oil

2½ cups white bread flour, plus extra for dusting and kneading

1 teaspoon salt

1½ teaspoons active dry yeast

¼ cup finely grated Parmesan cheese

1 egg, beaten

oil, for deep-frying and greasing

FILLING

1¾ cups cream cheese

2 tablespoons snipped fresh chives

2 tablespoons finely chopped fresh parsley

salt and pepper, to taste

1. Put the milk and oil into a small saucepan over low heat and heat until just lukewarm. Sift the flour into a large bowl and stir in the salt, yeast, and Parmesan cheese. Pour in the milk mixture and egg and mix to a soft dough. Turn out the dough onto a floured surface and knead for 5–6 minutes, until smooth and elastic, adding a little more flour, if needed.

2. Put the dough into a bowl, cover, and set aside in a warm place for 1 hour, or until doubled in size. Line two baking sheets with parchment paper.

3. Briefly knead the dough and roll out on a lightly floured surface to a 10-inch square. Trim the edges with a sharp knife and cut into 16 small squares. Place on the prepared baking sheets and cover with lightly oiled plastic wrap. Set aside in a warm place for 10–15 minutes, until puffy.

4. Heat enough oil for deep-frying in a large saucepan or deep-fryer to 350–375°F, or until a cube of bread browns in 30 seconds. Add the donuts, three or four at a time, and fry on each side for 1–2 minutes, or until golden. Remove with a slotted spoon and drain on paper towels. Let cool.

5. To make the filling, beat together the cheese and herbs and season with salt and pepper. Slice the donuts in half horizontally and sandwich back together with the cream cheese filling.

1

3

5

These donuts are great for a packed lunch or picnic. For a more luxurious filling, add some slices of smoked salmon.

Cheese & Olive Beignets

MAKES 32 | PREP 25 | COOK 25 MINUTES

INGREDIENTS

1 stick unsalted butter, diced
1¼ cups water
1¼ cups all-purpose flour, sifted
½ teaspoon salt
2 extra-large eggs, beaten
6 ripe black olives, pitted and finely chopped
2 tablespoons finely chopped fresh parsley
3 tablespoons finely grated Parmesan cheese
oil, for deep-frying
sea salt flakes, for sprinkling

1. Put the butter and water into a large saucepan over low heat and heat until the butter has melted. Bring to a boil, remove from the heat, and add the flour and salt. Beat thoroughly until the mixture is smooth and comes away from the side of the pan. Let cool for 5 minutes, then gradually beat in the eggs to make a thick and glossy paste. Beat in the olives, parsley, and 2 tablespoons of the cheese.

2. Heat enough oil for deep-frying in a large saucepan or deep-fryer to 350–375°F, or until a cube of bread browns in 30 seconds. Drop six to eight walnut-size spoonfuls of the mixture into the hot oil and fry, turning frequently, for 4–5 minutes, until crisp and deep golden brown. Remove with a slotted spoon and drain on paper towels. Keep warm while frying the remaining batter.

3. Serve the beignets warm, sprinkled with the remaining cheese and the sea salt flakes.

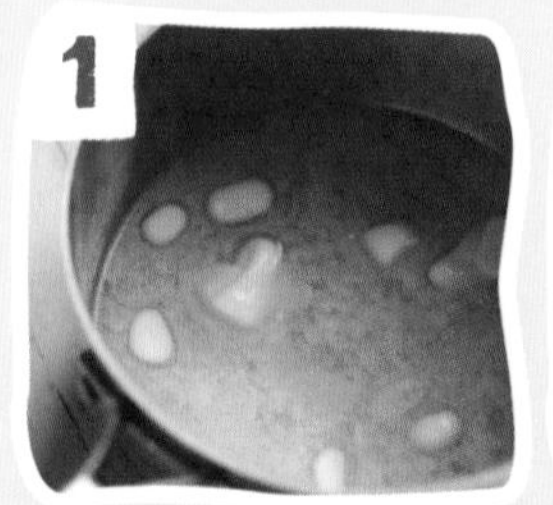
1

1

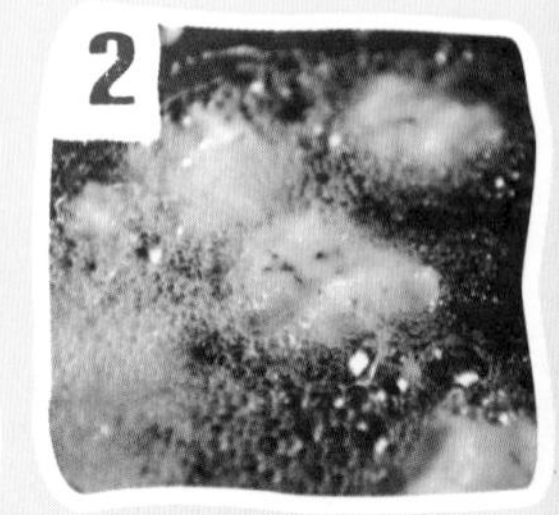
2

These light and crisp donuts are made with choux pastry. Serve as a simple appetizer or canapé.

Cornbread & Pepper Donuts

MAKES 6
PREP 20
COOK 12 MINUTES

INGREDIENTS

1 tablespoon butter, melted
1 teaspoon finely grated Parmesan cheese
½ cup all-purpose flour
2 teaspoons baking powder
⅔ cup cornmeal
½ teaspoon salt
¼ teaspoon pepper
1 extra-large egg
⅓ cup buttermilk or plain yogurt
2 tablespoons olive oil
1 scallion, trimmed and minced
3 tablespoons seeded and finely chopped red bell pepper

1. Preheat the oven to 400°F. Liberally brush the melted butter in the cups of a 6-cup donut pan, then sprinkle in the cheese.

2. Sift together the flour and baking powder into a large bowl and stir in the cornmeal and salt and pepper. Beat together the egg, buttermilk, and oil and stir into the dry ingredients. Beat until smooth, then stir in the scallion and red bell pepper.

3. Spoon the batter into a pastry bag fitted with a plain tip and pipe into the prepared pan. Bake in the preheated oven for 10–12 minutes, or until risen, golden, and firm to the touch. Let cool in the pan for 2–3 minutes, then carefully loosen from the pan with a blunt knife. Serve immediately.

1

2

3

Perfect for serving at a weekend brunch, these baked donuts are easy to prepare and take only minutes to make. They are best eaten warm from the oven.

Chile & Chocolate Churros

MAKES 16 PREP 20 COOK 25 MINUTES

INGREDIENTS

1 stick unsalted butter, diced
1 cup water
1¼ cups all-purpose flour, sifted
large pinch of salt
2 extra-large eggs, beaten
½ small red chile, seeded and finely chopped
oil, for deep-frying
¼ cup superfine sugar
2 teaspoon unsweetened cocoa powder, sifted

CHOCOLATE SAUCE

3 ounces semisweet chocolate, broken into pieces
½ cup heavy cream
½ teaspoon vanilla extract
1 teaspoon crushed red pepper

1. To make the chocolate sauce, put the chocolate and cream into a heatproof bowl set over a saucepan of gently simmering water and heat until the chocolate is melted. Remove from the heat and stir until smooth, then stir in the vanilla extract and crushed red pepper. Set aside and keep warm.

2. Put the butter and water into a large saucepan over low heat and heat until the butter has melted. Bring to a boil, remove from the heat, and tip in the flour and salt. Beat thoroughly until the mixture is smooth and comes away from the side of the pan. Let cool for 5 minutes, then gradually beat in the eggs to make a thick and glossy paste. Beat in the chile.

3. Heat enough oil for deep-frying in a large saucepan or deep-fryer to 350–375°F, or until a cube of bread browns in 30 seconds. Spoon the paste into a large pastry bag fitted with a large star tip and pipe four 4-inch lengths of the paste into the hot oil. Fry for 2–3 minutes, turning frequently, until crisp and golden. Remove with a slotted spoon and drain on paper towels. Keep warm while frying the remaining mixture.

4. Mix together the sugar and cocoa powder on a flat plate and toss the warm churros in the mixture to coat. Serve immediately with the chocolate sauce for dipping.

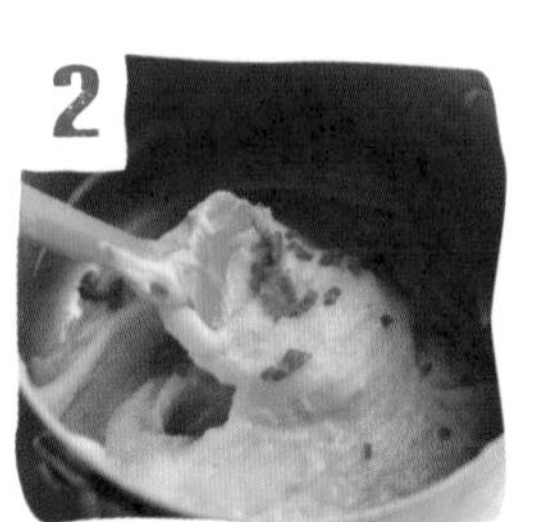

Chile and chocolate make a surprisingly good flavor combination. So be adventurous and try these classic Mexican donuts.

Spiced Donut Holes

MAKES 18 | PREP 20 PLUS RESTING | COOK 20 MINUTES

INGREDIENTS

½ cup milk, warmed
1 egg
2 tablespoons plain yogurt
1 teaspoon vanilla extract
1¾ cups all-purpose flour
2 teaspoons baking powder
½ teaspoon salt
⅓ cup superfine sugar, plus extra for dusting
1 teaspoon grated nutmeg
2 tablespoons butter
oil, for greasing and frying

1. Mix together the warmed milk, egg, yogurt, and vanilla extract in a bowl.

2. Using an electric mixer fitted with a paddle attachment, mix together the flour, baking powder, salt, sugar, and nutmeg. Slowly add the butter and blend. Slowly add the milk mixture until the dough is smooth and thick and resembles cookie dough.

3. Let the dough rest in the mixer for 20 minutes.

4. Heat enough oil for deep-frying in a large saucepan or deep-fryer to 350–375°F, or until a cube of bread browns in 30 seconds. Drop the dough, 1 tablespoon at a time, into the hot oil. Fry for 1 minute or until golden brown. Remove with a slotted spoon and drain on paper towels.

5. Sprinkle with superfine sugar and serve.

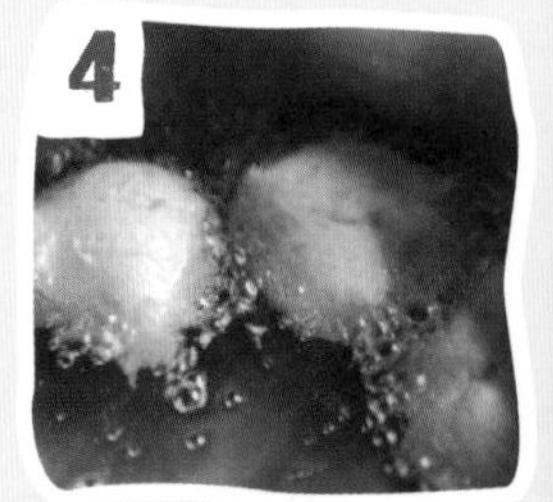

The nutmeg used in this recipe makes wonderfully sweet and spicy donut holes—the perfect mini treat!

Vanilla, Cinnamon & Chocolate Donuts

MAKES 24 PREP 60 COOK 30 MINUTES PLUS RISING

INGREDIENTS

2⅓ cups gluten-free, wheat-free flour blend

⅓ cup brown rice flour

¼ teaspoon xanthan gum

¼ teaspoon gluten-free baking powder

¼ teaspoon ground nutmeg

¼ teaspoon ground cinnamon

4 tablespoons butter, softened

1 cup ground almonds (almond meal)

½ teaspoon vanilla extract

1 egg plus 1 egg yolk

1 tablespoon buttermilk

24 gluten-free semisweet chocolate disks

1 cup confectioners' sugar, to dust

3 tablespoons ground cinnamon, to dust

oil, for greasing and frying

gluten-free chocolate sauce, to serve

YEAST MIXTURE

2¼ teaspoons dry yeast

1½ teaspoons honey

1. To make the yeast mix, add ½ cup lukewarm water to the dry yeast in a small bowl and stir in the honey. Let stand at room temperature for 15 minutes, until frothy.

2. Sift the flours, xanthan gum, baking powder, nutmeg, and cinnamon into a large bowl. Rub the butter into the flour mixture, using your fingertips, until the mixture resembles fine bread crumbs. Stir in the almonds, vanilla extract, egg, egg yolk, and buttermilk. Pour in the yeast mixture and stir well to form a dough, adding a little more water, if required. Set aside in a warm place until doubled in size.

3. Cover a baking sheet with greased parchment paper. Form 24 small dough balls and insert a chocolate disk inside each one. Place them onto the prepared sheet, cover with lightly greased plastic wrap, and set aside for 40 minutes.

4. Meanwhile, make the sugar dusting for the donuts by mixing the confectioners' sugar and ground cinnamon together.

5. Heat enough oil to just cover the donuts in a large saucepan or deep-fryer to 350–375°F, or until a cube of bread browns in 30 seconds. Cook the donuts in the hot oil, three or four at a time, for 2–3 minutes on each side, until golden brown. Remove with a slotted spoon, drain on paper towels, and roll in the sugar dusting. Serve with chocolate sauce.

These donuts are gluten- and wheat-free, so they are ideal to make for guests with these dietary needs.

Apple Juice Donuts

MAKES 12 | PREP 20 | COOK 35 MINUTES

INGREDIENTS

1 cup apple juice
2 cups all-purpose flour, plus extra for dusting
1 tablespoon baking powder
1 teaspoon ground cinnamon
¼ teaspoon salt
¼ cup packed light brown sugar
1 extra-large egg, beaten
¼ cup buttermilk
2 tablespoons butter, melted and slightly cooled
oil, for deep-frying
¼ cup granulated sugar

1. Pour the apple juice into a saucepan and bring to a boil. Boil for 10–15 minutes, until reduced to about ¼ cup of syrup. Let cool.

2. Sift together the flour, baking powder, and half the cinnamon into a large bowl. Stir in the salt and brown sugar. Make a well in the center.

3. Put the apple juice syrup, egg, buttermilk, and butter into a small bowl, mix, and pour into the well. Mix to a fairly firm dough, adding a little extra flour if the dough is too sticky to handle. Knead lightly until just smooth.

4. Divide the dough into 12 pieces and roll each piece into a ball. Flatten each ball in the palms of your hands to a thickness of ½ inch.

5. Heat enough oil for deep-frying in a large saucepan or deep-fryer to 350–375°F, or until a cube of bread browns in 30 seconds. Add the donuts, four at a time, and fry, turning frequently, for 3–4 minutes, or until crisp and deep golden. Remove and drain on paper towels.

6. Mix together the granulated sugar and the remaining cinnamon in a shallow dish and roll each hot donut in the mixture to coat. Serve warm or cold.

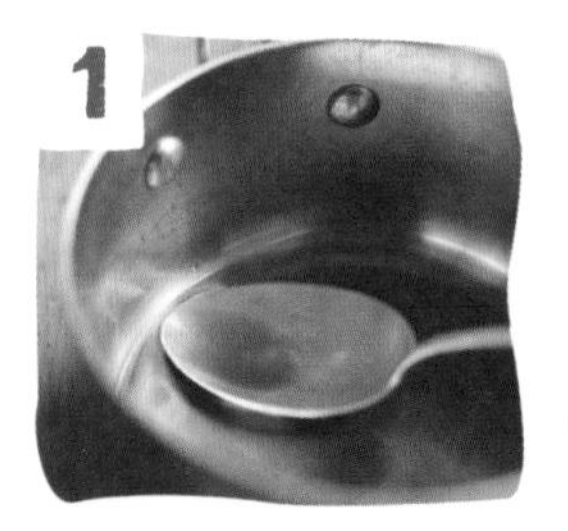

You can also make this recipe into ring-shape donuts. Simply roll out the dough, then use a round cutter to stamp out the rings.